JACK'S LETTERS HOME

Also by Cynthia Fuller

Moving Towards Light
Instructions for the Desert
Only a Small Boat

JACK'S LETTERS HOME
1917–1918

Cynthia Fuller

First published in Great Britain in 2006 by Flambard Press
Stable Cottage, East Fourstones, Hexham NE47 5DX
www.flambardpress.co.uk

Typeset by BookType
Cover Design by Gainford Design Associates
Printed in Great Britain by Cromwell Press, Trowbridge, Wiltshire

A CIP catalogue record for this book is
available from the British Library.

ISBN-13: 1-873226-85-8
ISBN-10: 1-873226-85-3

Flambard Press wishes to thank Arts Council England
for its financial support.

Flambard Press is a member of Inpress,
and of Independent Northern Publishers.

For my sister Pamela

Acknowledgements

I would like to thank Arts Council England, North East for a grant that allowed me to concentrate on the research for this book and its writing. I would also like to thank my family, friends and colleagues for their encouragement, especially Gillian Allnutt, Andy Croft and S.J. Litherland who read the final manuscript, and Tess Spencer for her consistent love and support.

Contents

France and Flanders: August 1917–May 1918

Afterword

Introduction

In May 1918, the month of my father, Harry's, twelfth birthday, his brother Jack disappeared in the course of a battle near Soissons, on the Western Front. Jack was 19 and a private in the 2nd Devonshire Regiment. His body was never found.

I grew up knowing that Jack had been killed in the First World War and that my grandmother had not recovered from his loss, dying shortly afterwards. My father would never speak about it.

In 2000, sorting through family belongings stored for many years in my sister's cellar, we found two wooden boxes. In one were more than fifty letters from Jack to his family. The letters were still folded and preserved in some of their original envelopes.

The letters are full of everyday details, the written word catching the chattiness of his voice. They document his path from shop assistant to soldier, his training from February until August 1917, and his time in France and Flanders between August 1917 and May 1918. Jack's story is his own, but it is also the story of all the young men who went to fight in that war.

My poems tell the story, drawing upon Jack's expressions and his tone. I create a voice for my grandmother as she endured his absence and wrote her own letters to her mother in Jersey.

Jack's name appears upon a war memorial in France. These poems are another memorial to him and all the other young men who did not come back.

Dear Jack

Inside the box
are neat piles of letters
still folded along
the folds you made
fitting them into envelopes.

Unfolding each one
smoothing out each page
my eyes travel over
the words as her eyes did.
I'm reading over her shoulder:

I find your voice
telling her what you eat
and where you sleep
telling her you are A1,
her loving son;

telling of pals, letters
every day from Win,
the new routines but
between the lines
how hard it is.

I glimpse your brother Harry –
he's eleven,
drawing cartoons for you,
missing you.
I almost glimpse William, your Dad.

Inside the box
crowd all the ghosts
from the house in Clegg Road.
They are still waiting
for your next letter.

Shop Boy

She tried to keep you safe
arranged an apprenticeship
with John Dyers of Southsea,
Outfitters, Furnishers,
Removals and Funerals.
It was 1915, April.
You were nearly seventeen.

Shop work was in the family.
It was clean and respectable.
She tried to keep you right.
You went with her to chapel
and did not drink or swear.
Still, she saw your Dad in you,
the passion for football.

You were a slight lad, not used
to roughing it, a shop lad,
neat and clean, polite.
You cared about your clothes,
about how you looked in
photographs, a family lad,
She tried to keep you safe.

Soldier

So many voices clamoured –
the mate who scorned your 'berth',
your comfortable shop berth.
Already at the Front he wrote
I don't think I shall ever go back
to the old job again as I intend
to go on soldiering if I come
through this lot safely.
He despised those 'hanging back',
argued for conscription.
There are too many of their kidney about.
Did you think he meant you?

420,000 killed at the Somme
while you took down orders,
ran errands, found time for courting.
Were you jostled in the street?
Did the whispering reach you –
too many of their kidney about?
Did you talk it through with her –
chapel rigour fighting with mother love?
The first letter, Winchester, Feb. '17,
Fancy me in less than 12 hours
in Kharki (S'wonderful).
Weight 133 lbs, Chest 35½.

I am told I shall be over in France in 6 weeks.
There's no need to worry now
as I am satisfied.
Am just what I wanted to be.

Training

February 1917–August 1917

To Mrs Drake, St Helier, Jersey
February 1917

Dear Mother, just to let you know
Jack's on his way to Winchester
to start his training.
We're all unsettled here.
William's been working late –
Jack spent a lot of time with his dad,
fishing on the pier, football –
now he can't seem to stay at home.
Harry is quiet – already drawing
soldiers and tents to send his brother.
The neighbours call round for news.
Jack is everyone's favourite –
a word and a smile for them all.
My head's been bad all week
but I'm keeping myself busy.
Teatime's the worst – he would
tell us stories of the shop.
How he could make us laugh!
We are waiting for a letter.

They Said

They said that I must let him go,
that war is just, that I must trust
in God, and send him off rejoicing.

I think how thin his shoulders are,
the milky skin, the knobs of bone
as he bends to wash his face.

I think how he stands at the mirror,
my sharp rebukes, his clothes
just so, his wink at his vanity.

Don't baby him. His father's words,
He'll be a mother's boy. My gentle son,
I pray you are not fit enough to serve.

I wait for letters, read and re-read,
try to see what he isn't saying
in his tales of boots and parades.

I try to picture him lining up
for 'fumigation', 'inoculation',
and all I think of is disease.

He says the meals make him sick.
I know shop work didn't fit him
for marching with a full pack.

He has learnt to use a bayonet.
He makes it sound an adventure,
even the drilling and cleaning of kit.

He writes of 'musketry' and I see
all the guns that will point at him.
You must be proud, the neighbours say.

Don't worry over me dear Mother.
It's worse at night in the quiet house
when I cannot find my faith.

A Soldier's List

A tuppenny tin of Bluebell
A tuppenny tin of Nutta for my belts and straps
A tuppenny Soldiers' Friend for cleaning my buttons
A letter from the girl
More stamps and envelopes
One of Mother's mince pasties
A walk by myself without my pack
A comfortable bed
An end to the rumours that we're off to 'India'
the 'hush' name for Mesopotamia
(I don't want to go there)
No more lads dying of measles and fever
No more fumigating, no more swabs
No more inoculations and festering arms
No more rotten throat, no more diarrhoea
A hot bath and clean clothes
A full belly and a light heart
Some cocoa and a bit of sugar
Home on a weekend pass

To My Best Girl

My dear girl, dear Winnie,
I've been reading all your letters.
How good you are to write so much.
It makes all the difference to me.
I'm going to slip out with this,
post it in the village, and look
for a cake or a decent bit of bread.
The weather here's turned off rotten.
It's blowing awful and proper cold.
I've been up since six, parade
at seven to eight in the snow
without anything in us.
Then after breakfast we could
hardly march for being so hungry.
Honest, it was cold as charity –
enough to make a chap break away.
I've never thought about food
so much in my life, and we've
hardly any – aint I an old baby.
Come on, Jack, where's your smile?

But what wouldn't I do
for a bit of quiet time with you.
Sundays like they used to be –
all clean and in my best togs,
walking along with you on my arm,
as pretty as a picture, my Win.
Don't tell Ma but there wasn't arf
a bust up here, a lot of chaps
got fighting through being drunk.
What a carry on – not me,
I keep my head down but
we aint arf a drunken lot.
Oh I do see life here, no mistake.

I can't help wishing I was back there –
but what I'm doing I have to do.
A proper soldier's life, not arf,
a bit different to the shop!
I think about you, wait to hear.
One day it'll all be done with.
I'll be safe back in Pompey with you.

To Mrs Drake, St Helier, Jersey
April 1917

We cheered ourselves up by packing a parcel.
Camp food is poor and Jack's short of money.
I baked all morning – mince pasties, apple pies,
cakes and buns – all his favourites.
We've sent paper and envelopes, pencils,
ink for the new pen. Wouldn't you think
they'd supply the lads with what they need
for writing home? It's a disgrace.
Harry wrote a letter – he's got a good hand,
italics so neat they make a pattern on the page.
He did one of his best drawings –
Jack training – just as he told in his letters.
He spent all the money he's saved
on presents for Jack – *The Joker* to read,
chocolate and sweets – he wrapped each sweet
separately – that will make Jack smile.
William bought *Woodbines*, candles and soap,
a new razor and blades, a tin of pomade.
We packed it up carefully, talking
all the time about Jack, and what he would
think of our parcel. Oh, Mother, I miss him.

Gospel Truth

You know I told you, dear Mother, about
the rough lot of chaps in this hut,
always swearing and carrying on.
Well, the night before last they saw me
reading my Bible and asked me about it.
Last night we had a little service on our own.
The chaps gathered round a table.
Most had YM New Testaments.
One read from James chapter two.
It was good to see them, and to hear them sing.

Then five of us offered to treat all the chaps
if they did not swear before Saturday dinner time.
Would you believe it, they didn't, not once.
It goes to show how hungry we all are.
We collected eleven shillings for a feast –
two large loaves, a pound of margarine,
a pot of jam, two tins of pineapple,
a piece of cake, two pounds of cheapest biscuits.
What a price things are – some feed eh, Mother,
it's the best feed I've had since I've been here.

You would have smiled to see some of
our company on the beach this afternoon.
They were carrying on like children.
Some of them never seen the sea or sands,
it was quite a bit of fun to watch them,
even walking in the water with their boots on,
daring each other to go farther out.
One picked up some small crabs, said he was
going to send them home to his mother.
(Gospel truth. I am not pulling your leg, Ma!)

To Mrs Drake, St Helier, Jersey
June 1917

Mother, Jack is coming home on leave!
He'll be here for his nineteenth birthday.
William has bought tickets for The Apollo.
We've got plans for Hayling, like the old days,
a picnic in the little wooden hut.
We've booked him up with the photographer,
so you'll have a photo of Jack in uniform.
You should see the card Harry is making –
a soldier with the Devonshire badge
on his cap – every detail correct.
I've been saving up, but prices are high.
He says this leave is a reward for
completing his training. Mother, I don't
believe he can be fully trained, not yet.
Pray with me that this isn't his last leave,
that they won't send him off to the Front.

Back to Camp

I'm writing this on the train, Win,
so excuse the writing.
I can't believe it's over.
I've been waiting and waiting
for this leave and it's flown.
I can't tell you how good it was
to see you, to have some time
alone, just the two of us.
I'm going to miss you even more
if that's possible.
Dear Win, you're the best girl
a chap could hope to have.
Don't I know how lucky I am.
Not arf, you bet I do.
But I didn't get the chance
to mention to Mother
the business about the ring.
The nearer it got to leaving
the more quiet and sad she was,
I just didn't dare.
She likes you, Win, I know that,
but it's me, not Dad, who goes
with her to chapel, reads
the Bible and lives the way
she wants – don't swear,
don't drink – Dad won't go along
with that and chapel means
so much to her, but he won't go.
I'll ask her in a letter
like we planned, if she minds
that your Ma has given you
a ring to wear when you go out
so the lads don't pester you.
I'll say you wanted me to ask.

She'll guess it means when I come back
you'll have my ring to wear.
You know how she is.
She likes things proper.
The night I came home on leave
she waited up for me.
It was going on for two.
She was at the table,
just sitting.

The Ring

My dear Mother it is good of you
to start saving for me so soon,
but there's plenty of time to put by
for my next leave – don't you go without.
Fancy poor old uncle Jack having
to go back in the trenches again.
He has done his bit – what a shame.
I want to ask you something, dear Mother.
I meant to ask just before I left
but owing to rushing round, I forgot.
Do you mind if Winnie puts a ring on
her engagement finger – her mother
has given her one. I meant to ask you
while she was with me Monday evening
but quite forgot it. You see, Win thinks
it would be better for her to wear it
as when she goes out the fellows would see.
But she has been worrying over it,
wondering if she is deceiving you
and if you would like it if you knew.
So, please dear Mother, write and let me know.
I don't think it is wrong, do you, as
I am sure it is a case between us.
Let me know as soon as possible.
I need your opinion about it.
I hope you will not be cross over it.
It's a lovely ring which her mother gave her.
I am sure you will not mind, will you?

Smile

Thanks for your kind letters
also for the photo although
I am not over struck with it.
Fancy my lips coming out like that.
I knew he took it too quick.
He ought to have told me about it.
Still, on the whole it is very good,
but I look like I am going to cry.
Isn't it funny, I generally
come out with my lips wrong.
I look too serious in it by far.
It looks like I am fed up with life,
and the best of it was I was so jolly
before I left to have it done, wasn't I?
Still, it is not too bad, but
I ought to have had a smile on.

A Most Lovely Answer

This is a proper tired Jack tonight –
a group of us had to climb up and hide
on Salisbury Plain – what a job in the heat,
full pack on, and it's almost upright!
The rest had to follow, try and get us.
When they got near enough they charged us,
yelling with bayonets fixed – some game!
Many thanks for your answer about the ring.
Dear Mother, that has cheered me up a lot.
I have been anxious for your opinion.
It is a most lovely answer.
I should have liked to give her the ring
but must wait a little longer.
I can give her one, as you say, later on
if all's well. Glad you like Winnie
although I always thought you did.
She does seem, as you say, a very nice girl.
I shall never never get a better one.
There is not a better one anywhere.
She is fond of me as much as I am of her.
We are proper in it as the saying goes.
You know that, the way I was always
with her, don't you, dear Mother.
You could not give me a better reply.
I will be easier now, but all else
feels uncertain, where we are going, when.
I hope to get home for Christmas
but I shall be very very lucky
if I am still in Blighty then.

To Mrs Drake, St Helier, Jersey
July 1917

Dear Mother, I'm sending on Jack's letters
if you would return them or keep them
until I come across with Harry.
How can they hope to train up lads when he says
The food they give us properly upsets me
and half the time they're starving?
He never was robust and now he says he's grand
then talks of tablets – opium and chalk –
and how his arm is swollen up and festering.
I'm sending pies and buns and what I can
but prices here are high now. I wish I could
send the three good meals a day he has at home.
He's not robust, nor used to heavy work.
You know how particular he is
about bathing and clean clothes and
now he hardly gets a bath a week.
He's joined the Young Men's Christian Fellowship
with meetings every night. He's a good lad.
I hope that keeps him right. I know he tries
not to worry me. He doesn't tell me
half of it, I fear, and how can I not worry.
I'm thankful that he writes so often and
thinks of us all. I have an eye out for
the post the whole day. Look after these,
Mother, and pass the news on to the family.
Pray for him and pray for me, your daughter
Charlotte.

Darling Winnie

It's rainy and dark here in the YM.
I'm trying not to be downhearted.
Sometimes all I can think of is you,
and home and the old life at Dyers.
It's not all roses here, I can tell you.
Haven't had a wash since yesterday.
What I wouldn't give for a shave,
clean clothes, all ironed, and you.
Had to do physical drill at 7 a.m.
with only a drop of tea inside us.
There's hardly any food in the camp.
I slipped out last night, down the village
with two other chaps – out of bounds
but I have to get out of here now and then.
Don't tell Ma all this, will you.
All weekend passes are stopped again.

I've been moved away from my old chums,
on account of being past nineteen.
You should see this rough lot.
Meal times – talk about a wild beast show –
three hundred hollering and scrambling.
They drink up their beer money, and more.
Not me though, no fear. I've had
a touch of the old diarrhoea again,
but that's nothing when they're dying
with measles and fever – don't worry,
we do get fumigated regular,
thirty at a time shut in a hut.
Enough to roast anyone, and we breathe
in gases supposed to kill the germs.
Talk about a job to get your breath,
it makes the tears come in our eyes.

They found the sergeant in charge
in the other hut is a carrier.
A boy, who was a fine specimen
for a chap of fifteen and a half,
was taken from that hut with fever.
Poor chap he is dead today.
His mother has not seen him
since he joined up. Isn't it awful.
Still, it'll take more than this to put
me off soldiering – you know that, Winnie.
Keep writing – your letters don't arf cheer me.
Go up and see Mother, if you can.
She'll be pleased to see you. I know she will.
Tell me about how it'll be when
this is all over and I'm back in Pompey,
back with you, my dearest, darling girl.

Welcome

I've nothing against her.
She's just a shop girl.
She dresses neatly enough,
that ring on her finger.

Each letter I get
says he's had one from her,
from *the girl – ain't she good?*
She sends a letter a day.

It was the word *darling*
that hurt, a slip of the pen,
darling mother crossed out,
changed to *dear.*

Well dear mother must draw
to a close as I want to
write to Win – writing to me
he was thinking of her.

Darling Win, my darling girl
is that what he writes her?
I tell him how well she looks
how much she enjoys herself.

It is so good of you
to make her so welcome.
She comes up on her half day.
He wants me to like her.

A Soldier's Wishes

That I've not had my final leave
That the girl will keep faith
That worry won't make Mother ill

That there will be enough to eat
That I'll be with some good chaps
That I'll get letters from home

That I'll be fit enough for it
That I'll be able to keep smiling
That war will be over soon

That my training will see me right
That my nerve won't fail
That God will see me through

No Fear

We must be moving at last.
First thing tomorrow morning
the advance party leaves.
They have sent a wagon
to take away the luggage
so I must be going.
In our company we're a poor lot,
just twenty percent fit.

But we are ready if wanted
and not afraid to go.
We've done all our training.
The chaps tied me up twice last night,
real tight, with three ropes.
We did have some fun.
You bet I got my own back.
It was a right old laugh.

Don't worry Mother
I shall be alright.
Am I downhearted?
No fear!

I was passed this morning
for General Service,
a fully trained soldier
ready when they want me.
We've done our bayonet fighting,
learned all the tricks, like
how to kick our opponents,
just throwing live bombs to do.

In five weeks time I've heard
we'll be going to France,
but the Doctor and the Colonel
are saying we're not strong enough
for the strain of modern warfare.
They don't want to let us go.
They can only find ninety fit,
just a half of what they need.

I was lucky to have had
such a fine week at home.
I wish I could see you all
once more before I go, but
it would make leaving harder.
So, Goodbye, dear Mother,
Goodnight and God bless you all,
your loving son, Jack.

Don't worry, Mother
I shall be alright.
Am I downhearted?
No fear!

Ready to Go

My dearest girl, it may still be rumours
flying about, but it looks like time's up here.
We'll be moving camp before leaving Blighty.
I know I am ready, my training's done.
But there's been a right old carry on,
with too many chaps not fit, too many
rushed through the training, and young lads
not sixteen some of them, a crying shame.
And who's turning a blind eye, I wonder?
It makes you think with so many needed
what we are getting into at the Front.
They had us practise how to fetch a man round
that has been nearly drowned because
a good number have been lost in shell holes.
And gas masks – I don't like them much – so close
inside, it's bad enough for a little while,
goodness knows what it's like for a long time.
Still, it's not all bad, you should see
the Black Watch and the Gordon Highlanders,
bagpipes playing everywhere they go.
Don't they look fine, and we'll go across
with them – no kidding, I might have a kilt!
I've written to Mother – go and see her
when you can, she'll take it bad, I know.
Dear Win, I don't mean to worry you.
I know I have to go and want to.
Our company's the oldest but sometimes
I feel how much there is I haven't done.
I love you, Win, and know it's right that
we've been 'proper' in it, as they say –
but wait for me, Winnie, and don't forget.
I need to know you're there, my girl
with your smile and your loving eyes.

Postcards, July 1917

They are giving it
to us proper now.
Proper stuff too
no recruits parade now.
No fear, we are men now.
Still mustn't grumble.

A pretty rough crowd
in this hut, not one
that does not swear.
It's real wicked
how they carry on.
Lance Corporal and all.

But don't worry
as I am alright.
I am getting used to it,
settling down a bit
I begin to know
what the Army is like.

*

We're in a camp in Norfolk.
They say we'll be picked out
for a draft next Tuesday.
Some Brigadier General
is due to inspect us.
How the people cheered us
all along the way here.
They thought we were off
straightaway to France.

It’s worse than the life
of a prisoner here.
We’re not allowed out,
we’re sleeping on the ground
on waterproof sheets – no boards.
Still, that’s nothing, I know.
If I came home with my head
under my arm I’d have
something to moan about, eh?

Last Stop

You bet your jam made bread and margarine
go down better, and I'm glad to hear
you've got a good crop of vegetables
and the garden is looking a treat.
I am orderly man all day today.
Just picture me here with cold water trying
to wash up greasy fat plates and tins.
How do you think I had to get the grease off?
I smothered them with dirt from the ground.
It's a dirty job proper and I'm sure
I got this today because I wanted
to go to Chapel, just my luck, eh?
Still, that's nothing. It's all disappointments
in the Army. And there's been an awful row.
This is a rotten camp – there couldn't be
much of a worse one – no water to drink,
men keep going sick – it's the food
and the way it is served – it's a disgrace.
We mean to get out of this somehow.
Our Colonel, the doctor and the officers
all say the camp should be condemned.
The Scotch say so too. It is really awful.
We had some big people down here –
big medical doctors – and our people
didn't arf tell them. They were at it all day.
But there's rumours that we won't be here long,
that we're to finish our training in France.
You know I don't mind. I am ready.
And dear old Mother, don't you worry.
I will look after myself alright.
Don't worry over me, there's no need to.
I could do with a few stamps and some soap
please, as I am nearly run out of it.
Fancy, I have not had a wash yet today!

France and Flanders

August 1917–May 1918

To Mrs Drake, St Helier, Jersey August 1917

Just a card, Mother, to let you know
Jack has been sent to the Front.
We don't know where he is.
Of course we knew it would be
but still hoped for a miracle.
Reverend Edwards has been round.
I know you will pray for Jack,
your daughter, Charlotte.

Living in Style

I am writing this in a place called
an *Estaminet* where I buy coffee.
It's like a public house in Blighty.
Out here they all sell beer – even houses.
I'm glad the silk card arrived safely.
They're a proper novelty – another is
the baths we have – grand shower baths, hot too.
We march to town, then in a motor lorry
to a proper bath place. We do live don't we?
In style too, taxis to go to baths in, eh?
I can get lovely ripe pears here, 3d a pound.
I went out last night and had a look around
then to a picture entertainment –
a New Zealand one – it was good too,
the first pictures I had seen in France.
Have passed my test tonight in bombing,
telling all about the bombs and how they're made.
I've got another test in throwing live bombs
behind sandbags – I hope to come out
with a bomb on my sleeve – swank then, eh?
Dear old Mother if you do not get
so many letters from me after this week
do not worry – I may not have
the opportunity to write so often,
so do not worry, there is no need to.
As you say, Mother, I am just the same,
cheerful and bright as ever, your son Jack.

A Bit Rough

I'm feeling a bit rough to tell the truth.
We had to dig a grave for four of our chaps.
They were killed by a shell as they rested
in a barn like this one, back from the line.
It was bad luck for the poor fellows –
one came over with us, one just back from leave,
one with leave this week, one a sergeant
in for a commission, just boys like me.
Our chaplain read the burial service
then we had to cover them. I suppose
I must get used to these things, bad as
they are. Poor fellows, I did feel sorry
for them, poor boys like us, and we shovelled
the cold earth over them, covered them up.

No Man's Land

Dear Mother and Dad, this is the first chance
I've had to write as we've been on the move.
It fell down with rain most of the way here,
the wind was something cruel, and mud over
our boots all the way, over our puttees
where we slipped in shell holes – it was that dark.
We did look a picture – tell Harry.
We had to stand in our wet clothes all day
until they dried on us, socks and all.

I am on guard in the front line,
on an outpost between Johnny and us.
You should see me halting chaps going by,
bayonet fixed – some soldier eh? I get
through it alright, although it's bitter cold.
We are out in a part of no man's land,
for the time being we're all on our own.
We look through a periscope, we watch
Johnny's lines, nothing but mud and water.

Food is scarce here. Your parcel will be
welcome – your homemade stuff, Mother,
will go down a treat, some pasties or cake.
It's dried up a bit today. It needs to.
We're promised clean socks every day,
and guess what to rub in our feet? – whale oil
to save frost bite. Just imagine the stink!
Harry will have a laugh at that – Jack
smelly feet. We could do with a laugh here.

So Horribly Cold

The weather has been simply awful.
It is raw cold and high winds.
What a condition the country is in –
nothing but mud and water everywhere.
I don't get much time to myself now.
Please excuse writing – it's raining,
my hands are so horribly cold.
But don't worry, I am still well.
As long as I keep so I don't mind.
Don't worry. Cheer up. I shall be alright.
Shall be glad to receive your parcel.
I can do with it, dear old Mother.
Am enclosing a letter for Winnie.
Please forward it on – I know she'll be
worrying if she doesn't hear from me.
I'm putting them both in this green envelope.
An ordinary one won't go so quick.
I know you will forward it on to her,
won't you, please, as I have not
written to her since I last wrote to you.
Am managing to write this on duty.
There are two of us on for two hours.
We take it in turns – the other chap
is doing his hour on now, keeping watch.
Well, dear old Mother, no more now.
Please forgive short letter, also scribble,
but I know you will understand.
Forgive me, won't you, my hands are so cold.
God bless you and don't worry over me.
I will keep writing whenever I can.

A Watery Moon

Your lovely parcel arrived safely,
everything in splendid condition.
The cake was grand and the pasties.
The pipe is a nice one, tell Dad.
Am enjoying a good old smoke again.
Thank Harry for those sweets – tell him
he is a good boy to think of me.
Will you send a pencil in the next one
please – that blue lead keeps breaking.
A good black lead will do, and some paper.

The sun is out gloriously today.
It turned off to rain just before dinner
yesterday and left off about three.
It kept fine last night for patrol
but the moon looked very watery,
as if we have got plenty more to come.
The trenches are still in a bad state
but as long as it keeps fine the water
will drain away a bit – I hope it will,
there's plenty about – and mud too.

That Gas Is Nothing

Please excuse scribble, but
am writing this laying down.
We cannot even stand up
in the dug out – it is so low.
We've blankets so we sleep
grand here by day, work by night.

Thank Harry for his drawing.
Tell him I do look a lad
with my gas helmet and hat on.
It's not the kind of helmet
he has put me in – tell him
it's a better one than that!

The vermin belt will be fine.
I put it on yesterday.
I need something – they are awful
out here, it is wonderful
where they all come from
and don't they bite too.

That gas is nothing, Mother,
don't you worry over that.
Didn't I enjoy a piece
of that cake at five when
we came back from patrol.
The other chaps had the buns.

We are some short in our platoon,
more fatigues and guards to do.
But we've new warm undervests,
gloves and socks – and leather jerkins.
Some soldier boy, eh, in a tin hat
and all – you wouldn't know me.

In the Pink

Thank you, Harry, for your letter,
your 'epistle' as you called it.
Nothing could be too long out here.
You don't know how we look forward
to letters, read them over and over.

This tank card I'm sending has been
in my pocket all this last rough time
in the line. You bet I've seen tanks now,
plenty, and those caterpillar engines.
(I've seen enough mud and water too.)

I'm glad to hear you're doing so well
at school – you know Mother worries you're
working too hard, taking hours over
homework, then doing drawings for me.
They go down a treat here, I can tell you.

That last one is very good indeed –
but *not true* – we leave them alone here
(what we do see) 'me noo like 'em!'
I won't need a dictionary, thank you
as people speak English pretty good.

I was glad to hear you are looking
after Mother, taking her about.
I know how she worries and I cannot
always write so often – you cheer her
for me, just tell her I'm in the pink.

Letters Home

It was the French schoolroom that did it.
Last time we were out of the line
I sat in a schoolroom at a school desk
writing my letters home.

I'd been laughing at the size of the desk
at my big soldier's boots, my legs too long
pretending to be a school boy again
writing my letters home.

A pain came like a wound in my side
stopped my breath, brought tears to my eyes
that I wasn't a school boy in class
writing my letters home.

All I try not to think about hit me
the chaps blown to bits and lost in the mud
the pictures that come that I cannot tell
writing my letters home.

Don't worry over me, dear Mother,
dear Winnie, the words I must say.
The censor would cross out my true words
writing my letters home.

I can't say I am frightened and sickened
by all that I have to do, I can't say
that I do not expect to come through
writing my letters home.

How I wish I could be that school boy
learning his ABC, a young boy
knowing nothing of shelling and guns
writing his letters home.

A Grand Parcel

My dearest darling Winnie
your parcel arrived safe and sound.
What a grand one it is!
I couldn't believe all the good things –
a pudding, a cake *and* mince pies.
I am lucky. And you are kind.
Thank all your family for me.

I'm sad that I can't be with you.
I kept hoping I might be lucky,
that I might get leave for Xmas.
But this last time put pay to that.
It's a shame how many we've lost.
We must refit and retrain,
with all home leave stopped.

You bet I'm not sorry
to be out of the line, I hope
for another week's rest at least.
It was real rough this last time.
I'm sad to say, our colonel
has died of his wounds – it's time
this was ended for everyone's sake.

But Win, I do try to keep cheerful,
so you cheer up too. Just think
we'll have other Xmases,
and our whole life together.
I'll think of you, you think of me.
This can't last forever.
I'll be home with you, wait and see.

Xmas Card

It's here and in splendid condition.
What a parcel! Thanks to Dad's packing
the box came a treat. A very nice cake,
the pasties just grand, you know I love
your homemade stuff – nothing to beat it.
I can't tell you how it makes me feel,
here in the cold night, miles from you all,
that taste of home in my mouth.

I've been rough the last couple of days.
Glad to say I'm on the mend – don't worry,
dear Mother, there's no need, by the time
you get this I'll be my old self again.
It's an awful puzzle how to keep warm –
drills and football games don't do the trick.
The pump in our billet is frozen,
frost thick like a fall of snow.

The mouth organ is welcome, tell Harry.
I'll miss our old singsong this year.
Never mind, we'll wait for the next one,
all being well, won't we have a spree!
Listen to this – *Somme* Xmas gift –
sardine paste and a tin of sardines,
a cake of Goodwin's scented soap,
twelve packets of cigarettes – no joke!

Have as good a time as possible
this Xmastide. I know how you will feel,
where your thoughts will be. Look on the bright side,
it must end soon for everybody's sake.
This card lists the battles our battalion
has fought in, and the sender of it hopes
for the next Xmas he will be home with you,
not on active service 'somewhere in France'.

Seeing the New Year In

We had a good fire in the tent,
a singsong and a smoke.
Johnny in his aeroplanes
was over our camp but that
didn't worry us, we still kept on.
After our rum issue I turned in at 9,
up at 3.30 for the new year,
breakfast at 4 and fatigues,
carrying barred wire, an hour's march.
There was a cold wind blowing
but the sun's out lovely now.
I had that turkey you sent for tea.
I did enjoy it, I can tell you.
New Year kisses, 1918.

Dead-beat and Done-up

Dear Mother, don't you worry,
but I am between the blankets now,
I have got what they call trench feet.
They are nearly double the size.
I cannot get my boots on.
Chaps have to carry me about.
It's some game, and I've plenty of pain.
They're so tender, can't bear a blanket.
Not much comfort here on
a waterproof sheet, on damp straw.
Proper rough luck isn't it,
but it's ever so much better
than being up the line.

It's the first time I've been dry, at least.
It gets you down – in our dug-out
we sat on cans watching the water
creep up our legs, over our boots.
We marched and marched in the rain,
water knee-deep, cold wind blowing,
dressing next day in our old wet clothes.
I'm not moaning. There's hundreds, no
thousands, of fellows doing the same.
I wanted to tell you, Mother,
to show what we lads put up with –
but it's ever so much better
than being up the line.

To Mrs Drake, St Helier, Jersey
January 1918

I'm sending you Jack's letters
with a heavy heart, Mother.
You'll see he's not himself.
He's been in hospital
with what he calls trench feet.
It seems his feet swelled
so big he couldn't walk.
But it's his spirit troubles me.
He doesn't sound like Jack.

He says he doesn't want to moan –
as if I might chide him for it –
then tells about the way
they're living day by day
(and that's without the danger
when they're in the line).

The rain, the snow, the mud,
the soaked-through clothes
they put back on,
up to their knees in water,
food getting scarcer, rations poor.
He sounds so tired, 'done-up'
as he would say. Poor lads.
We ask too much of them.

Keep the letters safe for me,
your daughter, Charlotte.

Lucky

Dear Win, it's been rough.
I'm out of hospital again.
It was none too grand there.
I know I'm lucky.
If you could see what I saw –
just young lads, some of them –
you'd know it too.
All I look forward to
is a letter from home.
I just hope I get through.

This candle I'm burning
is all shapes and broken,
but anything is better
than being in darkness.
Johnny is shelling on and off
all day – we were two days
in the reserve – holes in the ground
with waterproof sheets over them.
We had one fellow killed there,
three others wounded.

We've lost so many.
We're all dead-beat.
It's a wonder we lads
keep as well as we do,
with the cold and the wet.
The feet are not swollen now.
I can't see me getting
that leave I'm due.
Keep writing, dear Winnie.
I just hope I'll get through.

The Old Game

Am pleased to say I am going on fine again,
glad to be back at the old game.
Have been cleaning up all afternoon,
what with the remains of the mud
on my equipment from our last *holiday*,
and my rifle nice and rusty
from the wind and rain. Never mind,
it's all in the day's work, isn't it?

What do you think – your letter was opened.
It was censored, stuck down with G.R. on.
That's about the limit, I reckon, don't you?
It's hard a chap out here cannot have
a letter without it being opened and read.
No doubt there will be complaints made.
How cheering your letters are, dear Mother,
all we have to look forward to here.

To Mrs Drake, St Helier, Jersey
March 1918

No news still, Mother.
I go in and out all morning
looking for the postman, but
even when there were letters
I'd read, then start to worry
what might have happened since.
It's all I think of. I try to hide it.
Harry is a good boy, working hard
at school, then writing letters,
doing drawings to send to Jack.
He watches me, tells me stories,
even comes to Chapel with me.
I know the house feels wrong.
Don't worry, I'm doing the work –
I've even got the garden planted –
but I can't be cheerful.
I can see William is troubled.
I can't seem to take an interest.
I don't want him to talk about Jack.
I know he misses him – but
not like I do, not like this.
Reverend Edwards came to see me
but nothing moves this fear.

No More News

I received all your letters and all your cards.
No need to tell you why I couldn't answer them.
You'll have seen it in the papers.
Am pleased to say I am still quite safe,
and very lucky to be so – I've had
some very narrow escapes – but never mind,
I am safe, Mother, and I am lucky,
I can tell you, so don't you worry.
Am only writing a few lines
to let you know, am going to turn in
for a good night's rest – what a treat.
I had such a grand sleep last night.
I was dead tired and properly done up.
Am glad to say I am nearly myself again.
The weather has been pretty fair today.
Excuse short letter – there is no more news.

Prayer

Fight the good fight, we sing it still,
Onward Christian Soldiers and they are
our own boys, sons and brothers,
we see marching through gas and mud.

Chapel is filled with grief and fear.
We did our duty, sent them off.
Now we know the cost of it.
No letters come for weeks, the papers
report defeats and casualties.
They mention regiments, we scan
the lists afraid to find his name.

O Lord, you do not need him.
More than his country needs it
I need his life. Spare him, O Lord,
the best son a mother could have.

Sunday Best

All your letters were waiting
when I got back from the line.
You are a dear girl to keep writing
when you don't hear a word.

We'll get a few days now
then back in the thick of it.
I'm too tired to think.
I know you've been worried.

When I'm falling asleep
I have a special picture.
I always see you
in your Sunday best –

that blue and white dress
and your little white hat.
You're waiting for me
to walk up to Chapel.

It's Spring here – the flowers
make me miss you more.
Dear Win, don't forget me.
I'm your Jack, yours only.

A Soldier's Thoughts

I'm due home leave but we've lost so many.
They're drafting in hundreds, not even trained.
I can't see me getting leave – home feels far.
We had ten days rest. It wasn't enough.
Rations were scarce. We'd had non-stop fighting.
Chaps falling all round me – but I came through.
It's luck – shelling and tank fire in the rain and dark.
It could have been me. This time it wasn't.
What can I write home to Mother and Win?
They know we're in the thick of it.
I am dead-tired, dead-beat, done-up proper.
The order comes; 'Dig!' and I dig,
'Fire!' and I fire, 'Advance!' and I do.
Can't see me getting leave, getting through.

Alive and Kicking

Am writing these few lines before I go on guard.
I do hope you have had news of me by now.
I wrote my first chance, Mother, as you know
I always do. I know how you will worry.
And I receive so many letters from you all.
The sun has been out quite a lot today.
We went on a long route march this morning.
We did find it hot – properly sweat over it.

Thank Harry for his welcome letter,
also his drawing – he is a proper k'nib
and no mistake. Tell him I'm glad he is
going on well. Try to cheer up, Mother.
I know what you must feel like with no news
but it cannot last for ever. Remember
me to Grandma and all the folks at Jersey.
Tell them I am still alive and kicking.

Shall be glad to receive the razor –
will make the cost up when I do arrive
home – which I hope will be shortly now.
If I had been on my way home this time
they would only have called me back.
Never mind, I hope to be with you soon.
Roll on that time as I think I have earnt it.
Goodnight and God bless you, your loving son,
Jack

Afterword

To Mrs Drake, St Helier, Jersey
August 1919

Dear Mother, it arrived today
the official letter – a printed form
with spaces filled with name, rank and number
for the particular soldier.
I do not believe it.

30963 Private John Edwin
Henry Jeans missing since May 1918.
It expresses the Army Council's regret
at the soldier's death in his country's service.
I do not believe it.

Mother, I would have felt him go.
I would have known the moment he left us.
More than a year on, where is his body?
I cannot believe that this is right.
He is alive somewhere.

Don't you see, I would have felt him die,
and missing doesn't always mean dead.
He might have been wounded, taken prisoner.
Someone must know where he is.
How can I rest not knowing?

He is only a boy, only nineteen,
the best son a mother could have.
I feel he is still out there, somewhere.
Believe me, I would know if he died.
How can I rest not knowing?

22 Clegg Road, April 1920

They have gone with all their belongings.
William moved them in his own pantechnicon.
They have gone north to Kent to start again.
They took the bed he slept in, the clothes
he wore, the plates he ate from, the towel he used.
Like ghosts they drove away leaving behind
the sound of his voice enjoying a singsong,
his quick tread, two at a time up the stairs.
They left his cheery call as he set off for work,
his whistle as he returned each evening.
They took away with them everything they owned.
The empty rooms are thick with prayers and questions,
chill with the silence of unanswered pleas.

Family Tree

Harry, your brother, locked you safe into
silence he chose never to break. Your mother
wrote to papers, to generals, trying to find you,
only gave up after four years of waiting,
lost the will to keep living without you.
Harry watched his mother wasting.
He was not you. He could not keep her alive.

Your Dad remarried before he could miss her.
He ended alone in mad fits of wandering,
old man on the night streets searching.
Had they found your body they could have grieved.
Your letters stopped coming – the only thing certain.
Where did your life end, where are your bones?
All that's left is your name written in stone.